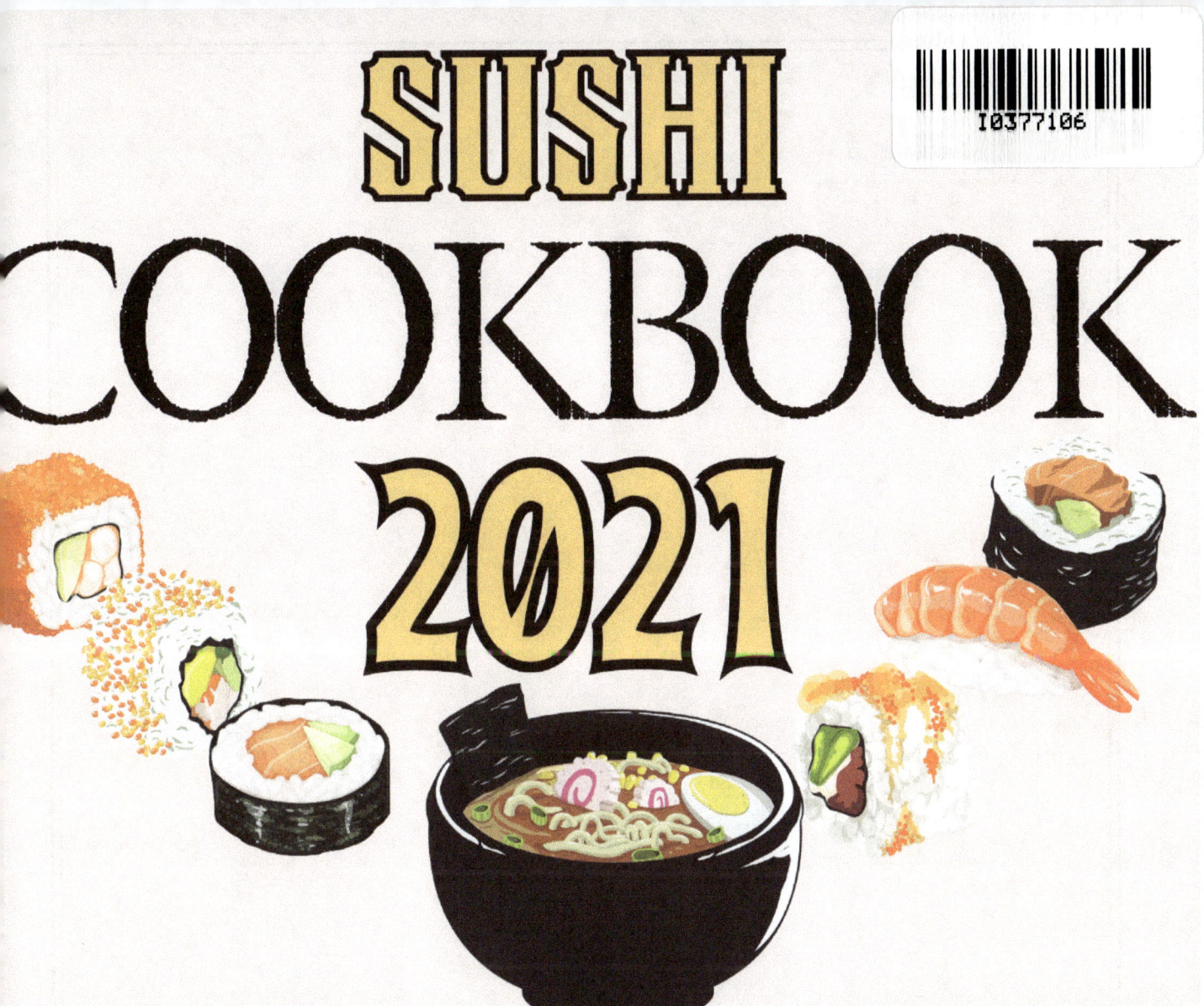

SUSHI COOKBOOK 2021

A STEP- BY- STEP PROCESS TO PREPARE HOMEMADE SUSHI LIKE AN EXPERT SUSHIMAN

-NIGIRI ACADEMY-

Nigiri academy

Nigiri academy

TABLE OF CONTENTS:

CHAPTER 1: ROLL RECIPES 9

- Mini Cucumber Sushi Rolls 10
- California Roll 12
- Cream Cheese and Crab Sushi Rolls 15
- Buffalo Chicken Sushi Roll 17
- Grilled Bacon Roll 19
- Mexican Sushi 21
- Avocado with Brown Rice ROLLS 23
- Smoked Salmon Roll 25
- Cucumber and Avocado ROLLS 27
- Sushi Party 29
- Barbeque Hot Dog Sushi Roll 33
- Turkey Roll 36
- Candy ROLLS 38
- Vegetarian Sushi 40
- Vegan Sushi 43
- Spicy Tuna Rolls 46
- Korean Sushi 48
- Inside-Out Spicy Tuna and Avocado Sushi 51

CHAPTER 2: DISH RECIPES 55

- Nigiri Sushi 56
- Sushi Bake 59
- SALMON CHIPS WITH ASIAN GUACAMOLE 61
- SEARED SALMON SASHIMI 66
- Spicy Sushi Dipping Sauce 68
- Garlic Teriyaki Edamame 69
- Deconstructed Sushi 71
- Tuna Carpaccio 73
- Tuna Onigiri 75
- Tamagoyaki 77
- Chakin Sushi 79
- California Roll Sushi Salad 82
- Tamagoyaki with Mushroom and Mozzarella Cheese 84

Smoked Salmon Poke Bowl	87
Ramen Slaw	89
Ramen Chicken Noodle Soup	91
Salmon Tartare	93
Tuna Tartare	95
Sushi Rice	96
Chicken Katsu	97
Nori Soup	99

CHAPTER 3: STAPLES AND SAUCE 102

Eel Sauce	103
Tempura Dipping Sauce	104
Sweet and Sour Sauce	105
Peanut Sauce	106
Homemade Pickled Ginger	107
Japanese Yellow Sauce	109

© Copyright 2021 by Nigiri Academy All rights reserved.

The following Book is reproduced below with the goal of providing information that is as accurate and reliable as possible. Regardless, purchasing this Book can be seen as consent to the fact that both the publisher and the author of this book are in no way experts on the topics discussed within and that any recommendations or suggestions that are made herein are for entertainment purposes only. Professionals should be consulted as needed prior to undertaking any of the action endorsed herein.

This declaration is deemed fair and valid by both the American Bar Association and the Committee of Publishers Association and is legally binding throughout the United States. Furthermore, the transmission, duplication, or reproduction of any of the following work including specific information will be considered an illegal act irrespective of if it is done electronically or in print. This extends to creating a secondary or tertiary copy of the work or a recorded copy and is only allowed with the express written consent from the Publisher. All additional right reserved.

The information in the following pages is broadly considered a truthful and accurate account of facts and as such, any inattention, use, or misuse of the information in question by the reader will render any resulting actions solely under their purview. There are no scenarios in which the publisher or the original author of this work can be in any fashion deemed liable for any hardship or damages that may befall them after undertaking information described herein.

Additionally, the information in the following pages is intended only for informational purposes and should thus be thought of as universal. As befitting its nature,
it is presented without assurance regarding its prolonged validity
or interim quality. Trademarks that are mentioned are done without written consent and can in no way be considered
an endorsement from the trademark holder.

CHAPTER 1: ROLL RECIPES

MINI CUCUMBER SUSHI ROLLS

Prep:
30 mins
Total:
30 mins
Servings:
12
Yield:
24 appetizers

INGREDIENTS:

1 long seedless cucumber, ends trimmed
1 carrot, shredded
1 (4 ounce) package cream cheese, softened
¼ cup raisins
24 long fresh chives for tying

DIRECTIONS:

1
With a peeler, slice cucumber into 8 1/8-inch thick slices lengthwise. Cut each slice into 3 pieces crosswise.

2
Place about 1 teaspoon shredded carrot onto the bottom edge of a cucumber slice; place about 1 teaspoon cream cheese onto the carrot, and press 2 or 3 raisins into the cream cheese. Roll the cucumber slice into a little sushi roll, starting at the filled end. Tie roll with a chive to secure. Repeat with remaining ingredients.

NUTRITION FACTS:

46 calories; protein 0.9g; carbohydrates 3.5g; fat 3.3g; cholesterol 10.4mg;

CALIFORNIA ROLL

Prep:
45 mins
Cook:
15 mins
Additional:
30 mins
Total:
1 hr 30 mins
Servings:
8
Yield:
8 rolls

INGREDIENTS:

1 cup uncooked short-grain white rice
1 cup water
¼ cup rice vinegar
1 tablespoon white sugar
½ cup imitation crabmeat, finely chopped
¼ cup mayonnaise
8 sheets nori (dry seaweed)
2 ½ tablespoons sesame seeds
1 cucumber, cut into thin spears
2 avocados - pitted, peeled, and sliced the long way

DIRECTIONS:

1

Wash the rice in several changes of water until the rinse water is no longer cloudy, drain well, and place in a covered pan or rice cooker with 1 cup water. Bring to a boil, reduce heat to a simmer, and cover the pan. Allow the rice to simmer until the top looks dry, about 15 minutes. Turn off the heat, and let stand for 10 minutes to absorb the rest of the water.

2

Mix the rice vinegar and sugar in a small bowl until the sugar has dissolved, and stir the mixture into the cooked rice until well combined. Allow the rice to cool, and set aside.

3

Mix the imitation crabmeat with mayonnaise in a bowl, and set aside. To roll the sushi, cover a bamboo rolling mat with plastic wrap. Lay a sheet of nori, shiny side down, on the plastic wrap. With wet fingers, firmly pat a thin, even layer of prepared rice over the nori, leaving 1/4 inch uncovered at the bottom edge of the sheet. Sprinkle the rice with about 1/2 teaspoon of sesame seeds, and gently press them into the rice. Carefully flip the nori sheet over so the seaweed side is up.

4

Place 2 or 3 long cucumber spears, 2 or 3 slices of avocado, and about 1 tablespoon of imitation crab mixture in a line across the nori sheet, about 1/4 from the uncovered edge. Pick up the edge of the bamboo rolling sheet, fold the bottom edge of the sheet up, enclosing the filling, and tightly roll the sushi into a cylinder about 1 1/2 inch in diameter. Once the sushi is rolled, wrap it in the mat and gently squeeze to compact it tightly.

5

Cut each roll into 1 inch pieces with a very sharp knife dipped in water.

NUTRITION FACTS:

232 calories; protein 3.9g; carbohydrates 23.7g; fat 14.4g;

CREAM CHEESE AND CRAB SUSHI ROLLS

Prep:
10 mins
Cook:
20 mins
Additional:
1 hr 10 mins
Total:
1 hr 40 mins
Servings:
2
Yield:
2 rolls

INGREDIENTS:

1 cup uncooked white rice
2 cups water
2 tablespoons rice vinegar
1 teaspoon salt
2 sheets nori seaweed sheets
¼ cucumber, peeled and sliced lengthwise
2 pieces imitation crab legs
½ (3 ounce) package cream cheese, sliced
1 teaspoon minced fresh ginger root

DIRECTIONS:

1

Bring the rice and water to a boil in a saucepan over high heat. Reduce heat to medium-low, cover, and simmer until the rice is tender, and the liquid has been absorbed, 20 to 25 minutes. Stir in rice vinegar and salt. Allow to cool completely.

2

Lay out seaweed sheets. Moisten hands with water, then spread the rice evenly on each sheet, leaving a 1/2 inch gap along one edge, lengthwise. Arrange strips of cucumber, imitation crabmeat, and cream cheese in a straight line along the side opposite of the gap. Roll the sushi from the toppings to the exposed end of the the seaweed sheet.

3

Using a sharp wet knife, slice each roll into 5 or 6 pieces. Serve with minced ginger on the side.

NUTRITION FACTS:

444 calories; protein 10.7g; carbohydrates 79.9g; fat 8.2g;

BUFFALO CHICKEN SUSHI ROLL

Prep:
25 mins
Total:
25 mins
Servings:
4
Yield:
4 rolls

INGREDIENTS:

½ pound fully cooked breaded chicken breast tenderloins
¼ cup hot pepper sauce
4 sheets nori (dry seaweed)
4 cups cooked sushi rice
1 carrot, peeled and cut into 4-inch matchsticks
1 celery stalk, cut into 4-inch matchsticks
¼ cup spicy mayonnaise
¼ cup French-fried onions

DIRECTIONS:

1

Mix chicken and hot sauce in a bowl and toss to coat.

2

Place 1 nori sheet onto a bamboo sushi rolling mat. Spread 1 cup rice onto the nori, leaving a 1/2-inch strip along one edge. Arrange 1/4 each of the chicken, carrot, and celery in a line near one edge of the rice. Use the mat to carefully lift the edge near the filling and roll tightly around the ingredients. Moisten the remaining edge of the nori with a finger dipped in water and press to seal; repeat with remaining ingredients.

3

Cut each roll into 8 slices using a sharp, wet knife. Top each piece with a dollop of mayonnaise and a small amount of French-fried onion.

NUTRITION FACTS:

522 calories; protein 14.8g; carbohydrates 54.7g; fat 26g;

GRILLED BACON ROLL

Prep:
15 mins
Cook:
35 mins
Total:
50 mins
Servings:
4
Yield:
1 roll

INGREDIENTS:

6 thick slices bacon
½ pound lean ground beef
1 tablespoon barbeque spice rub, or to taste
4 thin slices prosciutto
2 jalapeno peppers, sliced into long strips
2 sticks pepper Jack cheese
2 tablespoons barbeque sauce, or to taste
1 cup French-fried onions

DIRECTIONS:

1

Arrange bacon slices side by side, facing lengthwise, on a sushi mat.

2

Mix ground beef and spice rub together in a large bowl. Spread in a thin layer over bacon, leaving 1 inch of bacon uncovered on the end furthest from you. Cover beef with prosciutto. Line jalapeno strips across the end closest to you. Place cheese sticks next to jalapeno strips.

3

Roll up bacon tightly towards the uncovered end.

4

Preheat grill to 350 degrees F (175 degrees C). Grill bacon roll seam side-down over indirect heat until crisp, about 25 minutes. Brush some barbeque sauce on top. Continue grilling until barbeque sauce is glazed, about 5 minutes. Add remaining barbeque sauce; grill for 5 minutes more.

5

Remove from grill and coat evenly with fried onions.
Slice and serve with chopsticks.

NUTRITION FACTS:

660 calories; protein 21.1g; carbohydrates 28.2g; fat 49.4g;

MEXICAN SUSHI

Servings:
6
Yield:
6 servings

INGREDIENTS:

3 ounces low-fat cream cheese, softened
1 ½ tablespoons seeded and finely chopped chipotle in adobo
1 large plain flour tortilla
1 large tomato-flavored tortilla
1 large spinach-flavored tortilla
¾ cup low-fat refried black beans
6 tablespoons pico de gallo salsa
1 ½ medium (blank)s Avocados from Mexico, peeled, pitted and diced
¾ cup chopped cilantro leaves

DIRECTIONS:

1
Mix together cream cheese and chipotle. Heat tortillas in microwave or oven to soften. Spread each tortilla with 2 Tbsp. chipotle cream cheese, 1/4 cup black beans and 2 Tbsp. salsa. Scatter one-third of the avocado and cilantro on each.

2
Roll up tortillas tightly; wrap in plastic wrap and refrigerate. To serve, unwrap and trim ends; cut each roll across into 6 pieces.

NUTRITION FACTS:

332 calories; protein 9.3g; carbohydrates 40.5g; fat 15.6g

AVOCADO WITH BROWN RICE ROLLS

Prep:
30 mins
Cook:
45 mins
Total:
1 hr 15 mins
Servings:
4
Yield:
4 servings

INGREDIENTS:

1 cup uncooked short grain brown rice
2 cups water
1 pinch sea salt
1 tablespoon brown rice vinegar
1 avocado - peeled, pitted, and thinly sliced
¼ red bell pepper, cut into matchsticks
¼ cup alfalfa sprouts, or to taste
4 sheets nori (dry seaweed)

DIRECTIONS:

1

Rinse and drain brown rice, place into a saucepan over medium heat, and pour in water. Stir in sea salt, bring to a boil, and simmer until rice has absorbed the water, about 45 minutes. Let rice cool until warm; stir in brown rice vinegar. Rice will be slightly sticky.

2

To roll the sushi, cover a bamboo sushi rolling mat with plastic wrap. Lay a sheet of nori, rough side up, on the plastic wrap. With wet fingers, firmly pat a thick, even layer of brown rice over the nori, leaving top edge about 1/2-inch deep uncovered with rice. Place 1 or 2 slices of avocado and a small amount of red bell pepper strips and alfalfa sprouts in a line along the bottom edge of the sheet.

3

Pick up the edge of the bamboo rolling sheet, fold the bottom edge of the sheet up, enclosing the vegetables, and tightly roll the sushi into a thick cylinder. Dampen the bare nori edge with a wet finger and seal the roll. Once the sushi is rolled, wrap it in the mat and gently squeeze to compact it tightly.
Let rolls rest for a few minutes
before cutting each roll into 6 pieces for serving.

NUTRITION FACTS:

258 calories; protein 5.3g; carbohydrates 41.4g; fat 8.4g; sodium 89mg.

SMOKED SALMON ROLL

Prep:
30 mins
Additional:
4 hrs 30 mins
Total:
5 hrs
Servings:
6
Yield:
6 rolls

INGREDIENTS:

1 cucumber, peeled and sliced
8 ounces smoked salmon, cut into long strips
2 tablespoons wasabi paste
2 cups Japanese sushi rice
6 tablespoons rice wine vinegar
6 sheets nori (dry seaweed)
1 avocado - peeled, pitted and sliced

DIRECTIONS:

1

Soak rice for 4 hours. Drain rice and cook in a rice cooker with 2 cups of water. Rice must be slightly dry as vinegar will be added later.

2

Immediately after rice is cooked, mix in 6 tablespoons rice vinegar to the hot rice. Spread rice on a plate until completely cool.

3

Place 1 sheet of seaweed on bamboo mat, press a thin layer of cool rice on the seaweed. Leave at least 1/2 inch top and bottom edge of the seaweed uncovered. This is for easier sealing later. Dot some wasabi on the rice. Arrange cucumber, avocado and smoked salmon to the rice. Position them about 1 inch away from the bottom edge of the seaweed.

4

Slightly wet the top edge of the seaweed. Roll from bottom to the top edge with the help of the bamboo mat tightly. Cut roll into 8 equal pieces and serve. Repeat for other rolls.

NUTRITION FACTS:

291 calories; protein 11.1g; carbohydrates 45.1g; fat 6.9g;

CUCUMBER AND AVOCADO ROLLS

Prep:
35 mins
Cook:
25 mins
Total:
1 hr
Servings:
6
Yield:
6 servings

INGREDIENTS:

1 ¼ cups water
1 cup uncooked glutinous white rice (sushi rice)
3 tablespoons rice vinegar
1 pinch salt
4 sheets nori (dry seaweed)
½ cucumber, sliced into thin strips
1 avocado - peeled, pitted and sliced

DIRECTIONS:

1

Combine the water and rice in a saucepan and bring to a boil. Cover, reduce heat to low and simmer for 20 minutes, or until rice is tender and water has been absorbed. Remove from the heat and stir in the vinegar and a pinch of salt. Set aside to cool.

2

Cover a bamboo sushi mat with plastic wrap to keep the rice from sticking. Place a sheet of seaweed over the plastic. Use your hands to spread the rice evenly onto the sheet, leaving about 1/2 inch of seaweed empty at the bottom. Arrange strips of cucumber and avocado across the center of the rice. Lift the mat and roll over the vegetables once and press down. Unroll, then roll again towards the exposed end of the seaweed sheet to make a long roll. You may moisten with a little water to help seal. Set aside and continue with remaining nori sheets, rice and fillings.

3

Use a sharp wet knife to slice the rolls into 5 or 6 slices. Serve cut side up with your favorite sushi condiments.

NUTRITION FACTS:

171 calories; protein 3g; carbohydrates 28.7g; fat 5.1g

SUSHI PARTY

Prep:
3 hrs
Cook:
30 mins
Total:
3 hrs 30 mins
Servings:
12
Yield:
12 rolls

INGREDIENTS:

Rice:

9 ¾ cups water
5 ½ cups Japanese sushi-style white rice
5 ½ tablespoons rice vinegar
5 ½ tablespoons white sugar
2 ¾ tablespoons kosher salt

Filling:

1 teaspoon vegetable oil
2 eggs, beaten
1 tablespoon vegetable oil
1 tablespoon sake
1 tablespoon soy sauce
2 tablespoons sesame oil
1 eggplant, sliced lengthwise into strips
1 carrot, sliced into thin strips
1 tablespoon rice vinegar
1 tablespoon soy sauce
8 spears fresh asparagus
1 avocado
1 tablespoon lemon juice, or as needed
12 sheets nori (dry seaweed)
1 (8 ounce) package imitation crabmeat strips, halved lengthwise
1 cucumber, seeded and sliced lengthwise into strips
1 (4 ounce) jar pesto
8 large cooked shrimp, coarsely chopped

DIRECTIONS:

1

Bring water and rice to a boil in a large pot. Reduce heat to medium-low, cover, and simmer until the rice is tender and liquid has been absorbed, about 25 minutes. Remove pot from heat and keep covered for 10 minutes.

2

Stir 5 1/2 tablespoons rice vinegar, sugar, and salt together in a microwave-safe bowl; microwave until vinegar mixture is warmed, 30 to 45 seconds. Stir well. Add vinegar mixture to rice and toss thoroughly to coat each grain of rice; cool completely.

3

Heat 1 teaspoon vegetable oil in a small skillet over medium heat; cook eggs in hot oil until firm, 3 to 5 minutes. Transfer eggs to a plate and cut into strips.

4

Heat 1 tablespoon vegetable oil, sake, 1 tablespoon soy sauce, and sesame oil in a skillet over medium heat; fry eggplant in oil mixture until softened and lightly charred, 5 to 10 minutes. Transfer eggplant to a paper towel-lined plate.

5

Mix carrot, 1 tablespoon rice vinegar, and 1 tablespoon soy sauce together in a microwave-safe bowl; microwave until carrot is softened, 1 to 2 minutes. Drain.

6

Bring a large pot of lightly salted water to a boil; add asparagus and cook until bright green, 2 to 3 minutes. Drain and immediately immerse asparagus in ice water for several minutes to stop the cooking process. Drain.

7

Cut avocado into 8 slices and drizzle lemon juice over slices in a bowl.

8

Lay nori sheets on a flat work surface, wet hands, and spread 3/4 to 1 cup rice onto each sheet. Press rice into a thin layer, leaving 1/2-inch exposed nori on 1 long side.

9

For California rolls, layer crabmeat, avocado, cucumber, and carrot atop one another in a thin strip along the edge opposite the uncovered edge on 3 nori sheets.

10

For eggplant and avocado rolls, layer eggplant and avocado atop one another in a thin strip along the edge opposite the uncovered edge on 3 nori sheets.

11

For pesto and egg rolls, spread pesto in a thin strip along the edge opposite the uncovered edge and top with egg slices on 3 nori sheets.

12

For shrimp and asparagus rolls, layer shrimp and asparagus atop one another in a thin strip along the edge opposite the uncovered edge on 3 nori sheets.

13

Transfer 1 prepared nori to a bamboo sushi mat. Use the mat to roll the nori and rice around the filling toward the exposed nori edge, squeezing gently. Wet the exposed nori edge and seal the roll. Slice each roll into 8 pieces. Repeat with remaining prepared nori.

NUTRITION FACTS:

516 calories; protein 12.5g; carbohydrates 87.9g; fat 12.4g;

BARBEQUE HOT DOG SUSHI ROLL

Prep:
15 mins
Cook:
30 mins
Additional:
30 mins
Total:
1 hr 15 mins
Servings:
2
Yield:
6 slices

INGREDIENTS:

1 cup water
1 cup short-grain sushi rice
1 tablespoon rice vinegar
1 all-beef hot dog
1 sheet nori (dry seaweed)
1 tablespoon diced red onion
¼ cup barbeque sauce, divided
¼ cup shredded Cheddar cheese, divided
2 tablespoons French-fried onions

DIRECTIONS:

1

Bring 1 cup water and rice to a boil in a saucepan. Reduce heat to low, cover, and simmer until rice is tender, about 15 minutes. Remove from heat and let stand, covered, until water is absorbed, about 10 minutes. Stir vinegar into rice. Measure out 1/3 cup for sushi roll and refrigerate until cool, about 30 minutes.

2

Bring a small pot of water to a boil. Reduce heat; add hot dog. Simmer until heated through, about 5 minutes.

3

Lay a large piece of plastic wrap on a flat work surface. Place a cup of warm water nearby. Place nori 2 inches from the edge closest to you. With wet fingers, spread cold rice in an even layer over the nori. Place hot dog 1 inch from the bottom edge of rice and nori. Lay onion in a row beside the hot dog. Spread 2 tablespoons barbeque sauce on top of the hot dog. Sprinkle 2 tablespoons Cheddar cheese on top.

4

Grab the edge of the plastic wrap closest to you and lift the nori gently. Fold over, enclosing the filling, and tightly roll the sushi into a thick cylinder by pulling on the plastic wrap. Remove plastic wrap. Dip your fingers in warm water and lightly pat the edge of the nori to seal shut.

5

Cut sushi roll into 6 equal slices with a sharp knife. Transfer slices to a serving dish. Top with remaining 2 tablespoons barbeque sauce and 2 tablespoons Cheddar cheese. Sprinkle with French-fried onions.

NUTRITION FACTS:

629 calories; protein 12.7g; carbohydrates 98.1g; fat 19g; cholesterol 26.8mg;

TURKEY ROLL

Prep:
15 mins
Total:
15 mins
Servings:
4
Yield:
4 servings

INGREDIENTS:

¾ cup fresh spinach, chopped
¼ cup cream cheese, softened
¼ cup shredded Cheddar cheese, or more to taste
4 pickled peppers, chopped
½ spring onion (green part only), chopped, or more to taste
2 teaspoons garlic powder
¾ teaspoon ground black pepper
2 pinches red pepper flakes
2 flour tortillas
½ pound sliced deli turkey meat

DIRECTIONS:

1

Mix spinach, cream cheese, Cheddar cheese, pickled peppers, spring onion, garlic powder, black pepper, and red pepper flakes together in a bowl. Spread cream cheese mixture, about 1-inch wide, over the top portion of each tortilla, reserving about 1 tablespoon cream cheese mixture for sealing.

2

Arrange turkey onto each tortilla below the cream cheese mixture section. Spread a thin line of reserved cream cheese mixture below the turkey section of each tortilla for sealing. Starting at the end with the most cream cheese mixture, roll each tortilla around the filling, sealing together with the opposite end with small amount of cream cheese mixture. Cut 1/2-inch-wide slices from roll creating turkey 'sushi' rolls.

NUTRITION FACTS:

225 calories; protein 14.9g; carbohydrates 18.9g; fat 10.3g; cholesterol 46.3mg;

CANDY ROLLS

Prep:
15 mins
Cook:
5 mins
Additional:
10 mins
Total:
30 mins
Servings:
12
Yield:
12 servings

INGREDIENTS:

1 (10.5 ounce) package miniature marshmallows
2 tablespoons butter
½ (17.5 ounce) package crispy rice cereal
3 square fruit rolls
4 pieces red licorice

DIRECTIONS:

1

Combine marshmallows and butter in a large saucepan over medium-low heat; cook and stir until melted, 5 to 10 minutes. Stir rice cereal into marshmallow mixture until evenly coated. Remove saucepan from heat and cool mixture until easily handled, about 10 minutes.

2

Unroll fruit rolls onto a work surface. Cut licorice to fit the length of each fruit roll.

3

Spoon rice mixture onto half of each fruit roll. Place a piece of licorice on top of 1 rice mixture edge. Starting on the licorice edge, roll fruit roll around rice mixture ending with the fruit roll edge without rice mixture to seal. Repeat with remaining fruit rolls.

4

Dip a knife in water and slice 'sushi' into equal-size pieces.

NUTRITION FACTS:

208 calories; protein 1.5g; carbohydrates 44.7g; fat 2.3g;

Vegetarian Sushi

Prep:
45 mins
Cook:
15 mins
Additional:
10 mins
Total:
1 hr 10 mins
Servings:
4
Yield:
4 sushi rolls

INGREDIENTS:

1 ½ cups uncooked short-grain white rice

1 ½ cups water

⅓ cup red wine vinegar

2 teaspoons white sugar

1 teaspoon salt

½ avocado - peeled, pitted, and thinly sliced

1 teaspoon lemon juice

¼ cup sesame seeds, or as needed

½ cucumber - peeled, seeded, and cut into matchsticks

½ green bell pepper, seeded and cut into matchsticks

½ zucchini, cut into matchsticks

DIRECTIONS:

1
Place rice and water in a saucepan over high heat, bring to a boil, and reduce heat to very low. Cover with a tight-fitting lid and simmer rice until water is absorbed, about 15 minutes. Remove rice from heat and allow to stand covered for 10 minutes.

2
Mix red wine vinegar, sugar, and salt in a bowl until sugar has dissolved. Fluff rice with a fork and transfer into a large bowl; pour vinegar mixture into the rice and stir to coat rice. Spread rice out onto a large piece of parchment paper and fan the rice until cool. Cover rice with damp paper towels.

3
Sprinkle avocado slices with lemon juice in a bowl.

4
Spread a thin layer of sesame seeds onto a sushi mat. Pick up about half a cup of cooled rice and place onto sushi mat in an even layer. Place 1/4 of the cucumber, avocado slices, bell pepper, and zucchini in a line down the middle of the rice.

5
Pick up the edge of the sushi mat, fold the bottom edge of the sheet up, enclosing the filling, and tightly roll the sushi into a thick cylinder. Once the sushi is rolled, wrap it in the mat and gently squeeze to compact it tightly. Repeat with remaining ingredients to made 4 rolls. Place rolls on a serving plate, slice into 6 or 8 pieces per roll, and cover with damp paper towels until serving time.

NUTRITION FACTS:

385 calories; protein 7.5g; carbohydrates 69.7g; fat 8.6g;

Vegan Sushi

Prep:
30 mins
Cook:
38 mins
Additional:
15 mins
Total:
1 hr 23 mins
Servings:
6
Yield:
6 servings

INGREDIENTS:

1 cup short-grain sushi rice
2 cups water
1 pinch salt
1 ½ teaspoons vegetable oil
¼ cup rice vinegar
2 tablespoons white sugar
⅛ teaspoon salt
1 (16 ounce) package extra-firm tofu
1 tablespoon olive oil, or more as needed
¼ small onion, minced (Optional)
1 teaspoon garlic, minced (Optional)
¼ cup vegan mayonnaise

2 tablespoons sriracha sauce, or to taste

2 sheets nori, or as needed

½ avocado - peeled, pitted, and sliced

½ cup matchstick-sliced Savoy cabbage

¼ cup matchstick-cut carrots

¼ cup matchstick-cut seeded cucumber

DIRECTIONS:

1

Combine rice, water, and a pinch of salt in a saucepan; bring to a boil. Stir once with a bamboo rice spatula or thin wooden spoon. Reduce heat to low and cover. Cook until all water is absorbed and rice is tender, about 20 minutes. Let cool.

2

Heat vegetable oil in a small saucepan over medium heat; add rice vinegar, sugar, and 1/8 teaspoon salt. Heat mixture until all sugar has dissolved and liquid begins to simmer. Remove from heat and let cool until safe to handle, at least 10 minutes. Fold small portions of the cooled liquid slowly into the cooled rice until the mixture is slightly wet and sticky, but not gooey; you may not need all of the liquid.

3

Press excess liquid out of the tofu using a paper towel. Cut tofu into strips.

4

Heat olive oil in a small skillet over medium heat. Add tofu strips, onion, and garlic; cook and stir until tofu is golden brown, about 4 minutes per side.

5

Mix vegan mayonnaise and sriracha together in a small bowl.

6

Lay a sheet of nori, rough-side up, on a sushi mat. With wet fingers, firmly pat a thick, even layer of prepared rice over the nori, covering it completely. Arrange tofu strips, avocado, cabbage, carrots, and cucumber in a line along the bottom edge of the sheet.

7

Roll nori and sushi mat over the filling. Remove the mat and wrap the roll with plastic wrap, twisting ends tightly to compress the roll. Refrigerate until set, 5 to 10 minutes. Repeat with remaining nori and filling.

8

Remove sushi roll from the plastic wrap, slice into pieces, and top with the sriracha mayonnaise.

NUTRITION FACTS:

299 calories; protein 8.9g; carbohydrates 36.8g; fat 13.6g;

SPICY TUNA ROLLS

Prep:
30 mins
Total:
30 mins
Servings:
4
Yield:
4 tuna rolls

INGREDIENTS:

4 sheets nori (dry seaweed)
½ pound sashimi-grade tuna, finely chopped
4 tablespoons mayonnaise
2 green onions, chopped
1 tablespoon hot chile sauce
2 ½ cups prepared sushi rice
1 tablespoon sesame seeds

DIRECTIONS:

1

Cut off the bottom quarter of each nori sheet; reserve for another use.

2

Combine chopped tuna, mayonnaise, green onions, and hot sauce in a bowl.

3

Center 1 sheet of nori on a bamboo sushi mat. Wet your hands. Spread a thin layer of rice on the nori using your hands; press into a thin layer, leaving a 1/2-inch space at the bottom edge. Sprinkle with sesame seeds. Arrange 1/4 of the tuna mixture in a line across the rice, about 1/3 of the way down from the top of the sheet.

4

Wet the uncovered edge of the nori. Lift the top end of the mat and firmly roll it over the ingredients. Roll it forward to make a complete roll. Repeat with remaining ingredients.

5

Slice the rolls into 3/4-inch pieces using a wet knife.
Serve immediately or refrigerate until serving.

NUTRITION FACTS:

344 calories; protein 17.1g; carbohydrates 38.6g; fat 12.9g;

KOREAN SUSHI

Prep:
30 mins
Cook:
30 mins
Total:
1 hr
Servings:
6
Yield:
24 sushi pieces

INGREDIENTS:

2 cups uncooked short-grain white rice
2 cups water
2 tablespoons cider vinegar
2 leaves chard
2 eggs, well beaten
2 tablespoons soy sauce, divided
3 tablespoons water
1 onion, diced
1 tablespoon vegetable oil
¾ pound beef tenderloin, minced
1 (5 ounce) can tuna, drained
1 carrot, julienned
1 cucumber, julienned
6 sheets nori (dry seaweed)

DIRECTIONS:

1

In a medium saucepan bring 2 cups water and cider vinegar to a boil. Add rice and stir. Reduce heat, cover and simmer for 20 minutes, until rice grains are sticky and soft.

2

In a medium saucepan,
place chard in enough water to cover.
Bring to a boil, and cook until tender.
Cut into thin strips.

3

Whisk the eggs with soy sauce and 3 tablespoons water. Pour into a medium skillet over medium heat.
Cook until thickened. Remove from heat and cut into strips.

4

Heat the vegetable oil in a medium saucepan over medium high heat. Slowly cook and stir the onion until tender.
Mix in the beef and 1 tablespoon soy sauce,
and cook until evenly brown. Drain and set aside.

5

Preheat oven to 350 degrees F (175 degrees C).
Place the nori sheets on a medium baking sheet,
and heat in the preheated oven 1 to 2 minutes, until slightly crisp.

6

Place the nori sheets, one at a time, on a bamboo rolling mat. Line the nori sheets evenly with approximately 3/4 inch (2 cm) depth of rice, taking care not to let the rice cover the edges of the nori. Beginning at one end of the nori sheet, top the rice with a stick of carrot, a line of tuna, chard, egg, a cucumber slice, and a line of beef. Repeat until the food reaches approximately the middle of the nori sheet. Roll the sheets carefully and tightly. Seal with a grain or two of the sticky rice. Slice each roll into approximately 4 pieces and serve.

NUTRITION FACTS:

492 calories; protein 23.1g; carbohydrates 58g; fat 17.6g;

INSIDE-OUT SPICY TUNA AND AVOCADO SUSHI

Prep:
30 mins
Cook:
26 mins
Total:
56 mins
Servings:
2
Yield:
6 rolls

INGREDIENTS:

Sushi Rice:
⅓ cup Japanese sushi-style rice
⅓ cup water
2 ¼ teaspoons rice vinegar
2 ¼ teaspoons white sugar
1 teaspoon salt

Sushi Rolls:

4 ounces sashimi-grade yellowfin tuna, cut into small chunks

⅓ cup mayonnaise

3 tablespoons chile oil, or more to taste

1 tablespoon sesame oil

1 tablespoon sriracha sauce

1 green onion, diced

3 sheets nori, cut in half

½ small ripe avocado, thinly sliced

¼ English cucumber, cut into matchsticks

DIRECTIONS:

1

Rinse rice in a strainer until water runs clear.

2

Combine rice and water in a saucepan; bring to a boil. Reduce heat to low, cover, and cook until rice is tender and water is absorbed, about 20 minutes.

3

Combine rice vinegar, sugar, and salt in a small saucepan over low heat; stir until sugar is dissolved, 1 to 2 minutes. Pour over rice; stir until rice cools and looks dry.

4

Mix tuna, mayonnaise, chile oil, sesame oil, sriracha sauce, and green onion in a bowl with a fork, mashing to break up some of the chunks. Leave a few chunks intact for texture.

5

Cover a bamboo sushi rolling mat with plastic wrap. Lay 1 nori sheet, shiny-side down, on the mat. Spread a thin layer of rice over the nori. Layer avocado slices across the rice. Flip nori sheet so avocado is against the mat. Spread a generous layer of tuna mixture 3/4 of the way down the back of the nori; top with cucumber matchsticks.

6

Roll up sushi using the rolling mat, tucking in ends with the plastic wrap. Remove plastic wrap and place sushi roll on a plate. Repeat with remaining nori, rice, avocado, tuna mixture, and cucumber.

NUTRITION FACTS:

749 calories; protein 17.2g; carbohydrates 38.6g; fat 59.4g;

CHAPTER 2: DISH RECIPES

NIGIRI SUSHI

Prep:
1 hr
Cook:
35 mins
Additional:
30 mins
Total:
2 hrs 5 mins
Servings:
4
Yield:
4 servings

INGREDIENTS:

4 cups water
2 cups uncooked white rice
½ cup seasoned rice vinegar
1 teaspoon white sugar, or as needed
1 teaspoon salt, or as needed
¼ pound hamachi (yellowtail)
¼ pound maguro (tuna)
¼ pound cooked Ebi (shrimp), shelled and butterflied
6 eggs
½ teaspoon white sugar
⅛ teaspoon salt
1 teaspoon wasabi paste (Optional)
1 sheet nori, cut into 1-inch strips

DIRECTIONS:

1

Bring water and rice to a boil in a saucepan over high heat. Reduce heat to medium-low, cover, and simmer until the rice is tender and the liquid has been absorbed, 20 to 25 minutes. Transfer rice to a bowl and cut in rice vinegar using a rice paddle or wooden spoon. Season with 1 teaspoon sugar and 1 teaspoon salt, or to taste. Allow to cool to room temperature, about 30 minutes.

2

Prepare fish for wrapping by slicing against the grain into thin pieces about 2 inches long and 1 inch wide. Refrigerate until ready to use.

3

Whisk eggs, 1/2 teaspoon sugar, and 1/4 teaspoon salt together in a bowl. Pour about 1/4 of the mixture in a thin layer in a large greased skillet over medium heat. Cook without stirring until cooked through, about 2 to 3 minutes. Roll into a log and set in one side of the pan. Repeat with 1/4 of the egg mixture, rolling each log into a new log, to create one large log. Slice omelet on the diagonal into pieces about 1/2-inch thick.

4

Place a piece of fish or shrimp in your hand and smear it lightly with wasabi paste if desired. Grab 1 to 2 tablespoons of rice and roll it into a small nugget in your hand. Place the rice ball on top of the fish or shrimp, squeezing gently to make it adhere. Set aside while you assemble the remaining pieces of fish and shrimp.

5

Take a slice of egg omelet in your hand, grab 1 to 2 tablespoons of rice, and roll it into a small nugget in your hand. Place the rice ball on top of the egg, squeezing gently to make it adhere.

6
Wrap a strip of nori around each package; moisten one end of the nori strip and seal to join.

NUTRITION FACTS:

555 calories; protein 35g; carbohydrates 76.6g; fat 10.3g; cholesterol 350.5mg;

SUSHI BAKE

Prep:
15 mins
Cook:
15 mins
Additional:
5 mins
Total:
35 mins
Servings:
24
Yield:
24 portions

INGREDIENTS:

1 ounce dried shiitake mushrooms
cooking spray
4 cups cooked short-grain rice
6 tablespoons aji nori furikake
(seasoned seaweed and sesame rice topping)
1 (8 ounce) package imitation crabmeat, shredded
½ cup mayonnaise
½ cup sour cream
1 ounce tobiko (flying fish roe) (Optional)
1 kamaboko (Japanese fish cake), sliced into matchsticks
12 (2 ounce) packages seasoned Korean seaweed

DIRECTIONS:

1

Set an oven rack about 6 inches from the heat source and preheat the oven's broiler.

2

Soak shiitake mushrooms in hot water until soft, 5 to 10 minutes.

3

Meanwhile, lightly grease a 9x13-inch baking pan or glass baking dish. Spread rice in the prepared pan; sprinkle furikake evenly over the top.

4

Drain mushrooms and squeeze out excess water. Mix mushrooms, imitation crabmeat, mayonnaise, sour cream, tobiko, and kamaboko in a large bowl. Spread over the furikake.

5

Broil in the preheated oven until the top is lightly browned, about 15 minutes. Slice into 24 portions and serve in the pan. Spoon a generous mound onto a sheet of seaweed, wrap loosely, and consume immediately.

NUTRITION FACTS:

131 calories; protein 3.8g; carbohydrates 16.8g; fat 5.3g;

SALMON CHIPS WITH ASIAN GUACAMOLE

Time to prepare the recipe: 15 minutes
Time to cook: 10 minutes
Duration: 25 minutes

INGREDIENTS:

200 g salmon
2 avocados
3 tbsp. minced onions
2 limes
1 tbsp. mirin
1 garlic clove
1.5 tsp wasabi
Toasted sesame seeds
Soy sauce
2 tbsp. dices tomatoes
Rice noodles

For the avocado spice mixture:

1 tsp garlic powder
1 tsp dehydrated onion flakes
1 tsp cayenne pepper flakes
1 tsp cumin
1 knife tip of smoked paprika powder
2 sun-dried tomatoes
1 tsp Hawaiian red rock salt
1 tsp smoked rock salt
1 tsp pink Himalayan Rock salt

DIRECTIONS:

1

Preparing the salmon

Take a 200 grams piece of salmon (no need this time for sashimi grade). Sprinkle a generous amount of salt over the salmon on both sides. This will take some of the water out of the fish. It will also slightly change the texture and intensify the flavour. Store in a closed box for 45 minutes to 1 hour.

2

Preparing the guacamole

Put these ingredient into a (spice) blender:

1 tsp garlic powdor
1 tsp dehydrated onion flakes
1 tsp cayenne pepper flakes
1 tsp cumin
1 knife tip of smoked paprika powder (be very careful not to overdo it)
2 sun-dried tomatoes
1 tsp Hawaiian red rock salt
1 tsp smoked rock salt
1 tsp pink Himalayan rock salt

Blend all the ingredients until it's a smooth powder.

Note: if you don't have 3 different kinds of salt,
simply use 3 teaspoons of regular salt. Depending on the kind you use, it may be better to use 2 teaspoons. Commercial table salt tends to have a saltier taste than other varieties. Also keep in mind that you can always add salt later to adjust the taste, but you can never take away the salt once it's in the food.

3
Preparing the avocados

Cut two avocados in half, peel them or remove the flesh using a spoon. Cut the avocados roughly in smaller parts. This is not really necessary, but it makes it much easier to mash the avocados later. Put the avocado pieces in a bowl. Add 3 tablespoons of minced onions. Also add 1 tablespoon of the spice mixture.

4
Mashing the avocado

Mash the avocado mixture using a hand masher. If you use a blender, the result will be much too smooth. Guacamole should be a little chunky – but not too chunky!

5
Completing the guacamole

Roll a lime over the cutting board while applying some force with your hand. This helps release the juice. It's best to have another lime available, just in case one lime doesn't produce enough juice. Cut the lime in half and squeeze the juice over the mashed avocado. You'll have to decide for yourself whether you'll need to add more lime juice. Too much lime ruins the taste of the guacamole.

Now add 1 tablespoon of mirin (Japanese sweet rice wine). Some people replace mirin with dry sherry, but that will notably change the taste and is not recommended. Mix the contents of the bole by hand by simply mashing it some more.

Press 1 clove of garlic and add to the mixture. Also add 1.5 teaspoon of freshly grated wasabi. If you don't have fresh wasabi, use a bit less of the fake wasabi you probably have. It tends to be much stronger and can ruin the taste of the guacamole. Just add a little bit and taste until you like it.

Now add 1 and a bit tablespoon of toasted sesame seeds, a splash of soy sauce (1 teaspoon) and 2 tablespoons of dices tomatoes.Mix it all together, but make sure not to crush the tomatoes too much. The red of the tomatoes and the green of the avocado can result in a brownish color if you mix it too well.

Add a handful of coriander leaves. Not the stems, just the leaves. Chop and add to the mixture. Mix it again but don't crush the coriander, just mix it all roughly together.

Taste the guacamole. It should taste amazing! Cover the bowl with cling film and put it in the fridge. It will keep its nice, green color for at least a couple of hours.

6

Cutting the salmon

Take the salmon, rinse of the salt and dry the salmon using a paper towel. Put the salmon on the cutting board and cut it, keeping the knife parallel to the fat lines on the fish (the same as when you cut it for sashimi). Use a really sharp knife and cut of thin slices in a smooth motion.

Put some cling film onto the cutting board. Spread a bit of corn starch on the cling film. Put a slice of salmon on the starch, cover it with the cling film and press it, to make the starch really stick to the salmon. The salmon with the corn starch will feel weird when you touch it, but it is important to do this. It will help make the salmon nice and crispy.

7:

Deep frying the salmon

Put the salmon slices one (or a few) at a time in the deep fryer on a temperature of 145 °C (293 °F) for 3 to 5 minutes.

This depends on the number of slices you put in the fryer. Don't put it all in at once! The more salmon you fry at the same time, the lower the temperature of the oil. That will result in greasy salmon.

Make sure the salmon doesn't stick to the bottom of the fryer. Once the salmon slices float to the top, turn them around a few times to cook them evenly. The salmon should come out slightly leathery, not completely crispy. Let the fried salmon dry on a paper towel.

8:
Re-frying the salmon
Turn up the heat to 190 °C (374 °F). Put in all the salmon and fry for 3 to 5 minutes. This will make the salmon really nice and crispy. Then let it drain out for a short while above the fryer, to get rid of any excessive oil. Place the salmon on a paper towel to get rid of the last oil. Don't touch the salmon with your hands at this time, because it will be sizzling hot.

9:
Preparing the garnish
While the salmon is cooling, deep fry some rice noodles on a temperature of 190 °C (374 °F). The noodles will puff up and expand. When it all floats, it's done. Let it drain. You're almost done.

10:
Presenting the salmon and guacamole
Put two tablespoons of the guacamole on a plate or wooden board. You can add a few fresh coriander leaves to make it look even nicer. Place the fried rice noodles next to the guacamole. Add the salmon chips/crisps. Now it's time to taste the result of your hard work. Enjoy!

SEARED SALMON SASHIMI

Time to prepare the recipe: 15 minutes
Time to cook: 4 minutes
Duration: 19 minutes

INGREDIENTS:

1 Sashimi grade salmon filet
Pure sesame seed oil
Toasted sesame seeds
Korean spicy sauce
Fresh pickled ginger – to garnish
Watercress – to garnish

DIRECTIONS:

1
Preparing the Salmon
Place the salmon filet flat on the chopping board, and with a steady hand, lightly drizzle a conservative amount of sesame seed oil over the surface. Rub in the Sesame seed oil with your fingers, coating the salmon in its entirety. Turn the filet over and repeat for all four sides only.

Pour a small quantity of sesame seeds onto a plate, ensuring the entire surface area is covered. With your fingers, transfer the salmon filet over to the plate. Roll the filet over on the plate, coating all four sides. Avoid coating the ends, as they will need to remain exposed.

2
Searing the Fish

Heat a small quantity of sesame seed oil in a non-stick frying pan. When hot, transfer the salmon filet to the pan. Sear each side for 10-15 seconds – with the exception of the uncoated ends. Avoid overcooking the filet at any point, as this will cause the fish to disintegrate upon handling. Transfer back to the chopping board using a spatula.

3
Slicing the Sashimi

Position the filet horizontally on your chopping board. Apply firm pressure with your fingers to hold the filet in place, and with your knife, make a hira-zukuri (rectangular) cut approximately 0.5-1 cm (1/5-2/5 of an inch) in from the end. Simply align the heel of the knife with the top of the filet, and allow it to glide through the flesh to the tip. Repeat this cut for the remaining filet portion.

4
Presentation

Using a paintbrush, lightly paint a thick, diagonal line of Korean spicy sauce across the surface of your presentation plate. If necessary, add a second 'coat' for a bolder esthetic.

Slide the blade of your knife underneath the salmon slices, and supporting them with your fingers, transfer over to the plate.  Position the salmon slices diagonally on the plate, in the opposite direction to the sauce.

Add polish to your presentation with a pinch of pickled ginger set to the right of the salmon, coupled with a small heap of watercress atop the sashimi slices. Serve with a small ramekin of Chef Devaux's signature Korean Spicy Sauce.

SPICY SUSHI DIPPING SAUCE

Prep:
5 mins
Total:
5 mins
Servings:
2
Yield:
2 servings

INGREDIENTS:

2 tablespoons soy sauce
½ teaspoon chile-garlic sauce
¼ teaspoon sesame oil
1 pinch garlic powder (Optional)
1 thin slice lemon (Optional)

DIRECTIONS:

1
Stir soy sauce, chile-garlic sauce, sesame oil, and garlic powder together in a small bowl; add lemon slice.

NUTRITION FACTS:

17 calories; protein 1.1g; carbohydrates 2.1g; fat 0.6g; sodium 958.9mg.

GARLIC TERIYAKI EDAMAME

Prep:
10 mins
Cook:
10 mins
Total:
20 mins
Servings:
4
Yield:
4 servings

INGREDIENTS:

¼ cup water
3 cloves garlic, minced
1 (16 ounce) package frozen edamame in the pod
¼ cup teriyaki sauce
2 tablespoons brown sugar
2 tablespoons rice vinegar
1 tablespoon sesame oil
2 tablespoons sesame seeds

DIRECTIONS:

1

Bring the water and garlic to a boil in a saucepan over high heat. Stir in the edamame, and cook until the edamame are hot, and the liquid has nearly evaporated, about 5 minutes. Reduce the heat to medium-high and stir in the teriyaki sauce, brown sugar, vinegar, and sesame oil. Stir constantly until the sauce has thickened and coats the edamame, about 4 minutes. Sprinkle with sesame seeds to serve.

NUTRITION FACTS:

261 calories; protein 15.4g; carbohydrates 23.3g; fat 12.3g;

DECONSTRUCTED SUSHI

Prep:
15 mins
Cook:
15 mins
Additional:
30 mins
Total:
1 hr
Servings:
6
Yield:
3 cups

INGREDIENTS:

Rice:
1 ¼ cups chicken broth
1 cup jasmine rice
1 teaspoon grated fresh ginger
1 teaspoon grated fresh garlic
½ teaspoon salt
1 bay leaf

Sushi:
½ cucumber, cut into matchstick-size pieces
1 pinch salt, or as needed
4 ounces imitation crabmeat, shredded
½ zucchini, cut into matchstick-size pieces
½ yellow squash, cut into matchstick-size pieces
1 tablespoon toasted sesame seeds

DIRECTIONS:

1

Combine chicken broth, rice, ginger, garlic, 1/2 teaspoon salt, and bay leaf in a pot; bring to a boil. Reduce heat to medium-low, cover pot, and simmer until rice is tender, 15 to 20 minutes. Remove pot from heat and allow rice to cool, at least 30 minutes.

2

Place cucumber in a bowl and sprinkle 1 pinch salt over cucumber.

3

Mix crabmeat, cucumber, zucchini, squash, and sesame seeds into rice mixture.

NUTRITION FACTS:

152 calories; protein 4.5g; carbohydrates 31.1g; fat 1g; cholesterol 4.8mg;

TUNA CARPACCIO

Prep:
30 mins
Total:
30 mins
Servings:
5
Yield:
5 servings

INGREDIENTS:

1 (1 pound) loaf French bread
10 ounces ahi (yellowfin) tuna, sushi-grade - sliced 1 inch long and 1/8 inch thick
¼ cup onion, cut into 1/8-inch dice
2 tablespoons capers, drained
3 ounces olive oil
3 tablespoons fresh lemon juice
1 teaspoon kosher salt
¼ teaspoon freshly ground black pepper

DIRECTIONS:

1

Slice the French bread 1/4 inch thick, and set aside.

2

Place the tuna slices in a single layer in a flat nonreactive dish. Sprinkle the tuna with onion and capers; drizzle with olive oil and lemon juice. Sprinkle with kosher salt and black pepper.

3

Serve slices of tuna on sliced French bread.

NUTRITION FACTS:

477 calories; protein 24g; carbohydrates 52.3g; fat 19.3g; cholesterol 25.5mg;

TUNA ONIGIRI

Prep:
30 mins
Cook:
20 mins
Additional:
25 mins
Total:
1 hr 15 mins
Servings:
3
Yield:
3 onigiri

INGREDIENTS:

1 cup short-grain sushi rice
1 ¼ cups water
1 pinch salt (Optional)
1 (5 ounce) can tuna, drained
2 tablespoons mayonnaise, or to taste
1 pinch ground black pepper
1 sheet nori, cut into 1-inch strips, or desired width

DIRECTIONS:

1

Place rice in a bowl with fresh water. Stir until water becomes cloudy; drain and rinse. Repeat with fresh water until water no longer clouds, 2 or 3 times more.

2

Bring 1 1/4 cups water, rice, and salt to a boil in a saucepan; reduce heat to low. Cover and simmer, lifting lid no more than once, until water is absorbed, about 20 minutes. Remove from heat and set aside to finish cooking, about 10 minutes more. Remove cover and cool rice until no longer hot to the touch, about 15 minutes.

3

Mix tuna, mayonnaise, and pepper together in a bowl until no large chunks remain. Arrange nori strips on a serving platter.

4

Lay a 10-inch sheet of plastic wrap on a work surface. Place 1/2 cup cooked rice in the center, form a well in the middle, and fill well with 1 teaspoon tuna mixture. Top with another 1/2 cup rice. Gather edges of plastic wrap together over rice mixture, twist together to tighten, and shape rice mixture into a pyramid shape. Remove plastic wrap and gently place onto nori strip, with nori edges protruding (for use as handles when eating). Repeat with remaining rice and tuna mixture.

NUTRITION FACTS:

355 calories; protein 15.2g; carbohydrates 53.3g; fat 8g; cholesterol 16.1mg;

TAMAGOYAKI

Prep:
10 mins
Cook:
10 mins
Additional:
5 mins
Total:
25 mins
Servings:
2
Yield:
6 pieces

INGREDIENTS:

4 eggs
4 tablespoons prepared dashi stock
1 tablespoon white sugar
1 teaspoon mirin (Japanese sweet wine)
½ teaspoon soy sauce
½ tablespoon vegetable oil

DIRECTIONS:

1

Whisk eggs, dashi stock, sugar, mirin, and soy sauce together in a bowl.

2

Heat 1/3 of the oil in a large nonstick skillet over medium-high heat. Add about 1/3 of the egg mixture and quickly swirl the pan to evenly cover the bottom. Start rolling up the omelette from one side to the other as soon as it is set.

3

Keep the roll to one side, then add another 1/3 of the oil to the skillet and another 1/3 of the egg. Swirl the pan, ensuring the entire bottom is covered, including around and underneath the first roll. Cook until set. Roll up from the side containing the first roll, so that is now at the center.

4

Repeat the process with the remaining oil and egg. Transfer rolled omelette to a bamboo rolling mat. Roll up tightly and allow to cool for a few minutes.

5

Unwrap the omelette and slice into 6 pieces. Serve warm or cold.

NUTRITION FACTS:

209 calories; protein 13.3g; carbohydrates 7.9g; fat 13.6g;

CHAKIN SUSHI

Prep:
30 mins
Cook:
25 mins
Total:
55 mins
Servings:
6
Yield:
6 pieces

INGREDIENTS:

1 cup sushi rice, or Japanese short-grain white rice
3 eggs, beaten
¼ teaspoon salt
1 tablespoon vegetable oil
3 tablespoons rice vinegar
2 tablespoons white sugar
1 teaspoon salt
2 tablespoons black sesame seeds
6 sprigs Italian parsley with long stems

DIRECTIONS:

1

In a saucepan bring water to a boil. Add rice and stir. Reduce heat, cover and simmer for 20 minutes. Once cooked, spoon rice into a large bowl and allow to cool until it is cool enough to handle.

2

Meanwhile, beat eggs together with 1/4 teaspoon salt. Brush the bottom of a skillet with vegetable oil, and place over medium heat. Once hot, pour in 1/6 of the egg mixture and spread evenly over the bottom of the pan. Cook until the egg has just firmed, then carefully flip over and cook for a few more seconds to firm the other side. Repeat with remaining egg to create 6 thin sheets.

3

Stir together vinegar, sugar, and 1 teaspoon salt in a small bowl. Microwave for a few seconds until the mixture is hot; stir until the sugar has dissolved. Fold vinegar and sesame seeds into warm rice.

4

To assemble, place a large spoonful of rice into the center of each egg sheet.
Fold into a square, and tie with a sprig of Italian parsley to secure.

NUTRITION FACTS:

218 calories; protein 6.7g; carbohydrates 33.2g; fat 6.7g;

California Roll Sushi Salad

Prep:
20 mins
Cook:
25 mins
Additional:
15 mins
Total:
1 hr
Servings:
2
Yield:
2 servings

INGREDIENTS:

1 cup water
½ cup uncooked short-grain white rice
¼ cup rice wine vinegar
2 tablespoons pickled ginger, with juice
1 tablespoon mayonnaise
1 tablespoon soy sauce
1 tablespoon white sugar
2 teaspoons wasabi powder, or to taste
1 teaspoon sesame oil
2 cups shredded imitation crabmeat
1 avocado, cubed
½ English cucumber, cut into 1-inch strips
3 sheets nori, crumbled

DIRECTIONS:

1

Bring water and rice to a boil in a small saucepan. Reduce heat to low, cover, and simmer until rice is tender, about 20 minutes. Let cool, about 15 minutes.

2

Stir rice wine vinegar, pickled ginger juice, mayonnaise, soy sauce, sugar, wasabi powder, and sesame oil together in a bowl. Pour over cooled rice; mix to coat and break up clumps.

3

Dice pickled ginger. Fold ginger, crabmeat, avocado, cucumber, and nori gently into rice. Chill until serving.

NUTRITION FACTS:

637 calories; protein 19.6g; carbohydrates 88.5g; fat 23.8g; cholesterol 36.6mg;

Tamagoyaki with Mushroom and Mozzarella Cheese

Prep:
15 mins
Cook:
10 mins
Additional:
5 mins
Total:
30 mins
Servings:
2
Yield:
2 serving

INGREDIENTS:

2 teaspoons olive oil
6 button mushrooms, sliced very thin
3 eggs
2 ½ tablespoons white sugar
1 pinch salt and ground black pepper to taste
¼ teaspoon red chile powder, or to taste
2 tablespoons vegetable oil, divided
1 ounce mozzarella cheese, sliced very thin

DIRECTIONS:

1

Heat olive oil in a large skillet over medium heat. Add mushrooms; cook and stir until mushrooms are browned and release their moisture, about 5 minutes. Remove from heat, drain, and pat dry.

2

Beat eggs, sugar, salt, pepper, and red chile powder together in a bowl.

3

Coat the skillet with some vegetable oil; set over medium heat. Pour in some of the beaten eggs, tilting skillet to spread into a thin layer. Cook until almost set, 1 to 2 minutes. Run a heatproof rubber spatula around the edges to loosen. Cover with some mushrooms; roll up egg and move to the side of the skillet.

4

Grease skillet with some more vegetable oil. Pour in more eggs to create a second layer. Lift the first roll up to get raw egg underneath. Sprinkle mozzarella cheese on top; roll second layer up over the first.

5

Repeat layering and rolling process with remaining oil, eggs, mushrooms, and mozzarella cheese. Cook finished tamagoyaki until lightly browned, about 30 seconds per side.

6

Transfer tamagoyaki to a cutting board. Let cool for 5 to 10 minutes before slicing.

NUTRITION FACTS:

378 calories; protein 14.5g; carbohydrates 18.4g; fat 28.3g;

SMOKED SALMON POKE BOWL

Prep:
15 mins
Additional:
30 mins
Total:
45 mins
Servings:
4
Yield:
4 servings

INGREDIENTS:

¼ cup soy sauce
3 green onions, thinly sliced
1 tablespoon black sesame oil
1 tablespoon rice vinegar
1 teaspoon grated ginger
½ teaspoon garlic, minced
12 ounces smoked salmon, chopped
2 cups cooked brown rice
¼ cup diced mango
¼ cup diced cucumber
¼ cup diced avocado
¼ cup sliced fresh strawberries
1 teaspoon black sesame seeds, or to taste

DIRECTIONS:

1
Combine soy sauce, green onions, sesame oil, rice vinegar, ginger, and garlic in a bowl. Mix until thoroughly combined. Add salmon and marinate in the refrigerator for 30 minutes to 1 hour.

2
Divide brown rice among 4 serving bowls. Top with salmon, mango, cucumber, avocado, and strawberries. Sprinkle black sesame seeds on top.

NUTRITION FACTS:

283 calories; protein 19.8g; carbohydrates 28.5g; fat 9.9g;

RAMEN SLAW

Prep:
15 mins
Additional:
1 hr 30 mins
Total:
1 hr 45 mins
Servings:
8
Yield:
8 servings

INGREDIENTS:

1 (12 ounce) package broccoli coleslaw mix
½ cup sunflower seeds
½ cup slivered almonds
1 (3 ounce) package Oriental-flavored ramen noodles, broken into small pieces
½ cup canola oil
¼ cup white sugar
¼ cup white wine vinegar
4 green onions, chopped

DIRECTIONS:
1

Combine broccoli coleslaw mix, sunflower seeds, almonds, and ramen noodles together in a bowl. Whisk canola oil, sugar, ramen noodle seasoning packet, and vinegar together in a separate bowl; pour over slaw mixture. Fold in green onions. Chill in refrigerator for 1 1/2 hours before serving.

NUTRITION FACTS:

302 calories; protein 4.6g; carbohydrates 19g; fat 23.8g;

RAMEN CHICKEN NOODLE SOUP

Prep:
5 mins
Additional:
20 mins
Total:
25 mins
Servings:
4
Yield:
4 servings

INGREDIENTS:

3 ½ cups Chicken Broth
1 teaspoon soy sauce
1 teaspoon ground ginger
1 dash black pepper
1 medium carrot, sliced diagonally
1 stalk celery, sliced diagonally
½ red bell pepper, cut into 2-inch-long strips
2 green onions, sliced diagonally
1 clove garlic, minced
4 ounces broken-up uncooked ramen noodles
1 cup cooked, shredded boneless, skinless chicken breast meat

DIRECTIONS:

tep 1
Heat the broth, soy sauce, ginger, black pepper, carrot, celery, red pepper, green onions and garlic in a 2-quart saucepan over medium-high heat to a boil.

2
Stir the noodles and chicken in the saucepan. Reduce the heat to medium and cook for 10 minutes or until the noodles are done.

NUTRITION FACTS:

111 calories; protein 11.6g; carbohydrates 7.4g; fat 4g;

SALMON TARTARE

Prep:
10 mins
Additional:
5 mins
Total:
15 mins
Servings:
2
Yield:
2 servings

INGREDIENTS:

1 (5 ounce) very fresh salmon fillet
1 teaspoon minced shallot
1 teaspoon minced fresh flat-leaf parsley
1 teaspoon minced fresh chives
1 teaspoon minced cornichon (small pickled cucumber)
1 teaspoon fresh lemon juice, or more to taste
sea salt and freshly ground black pepper to taste

DIRECTIONS:

1

Remove salmon skin and cut out the grey colored blood line so you have only the shiny pink flesh. Cut salmon into small cubes and place in a bowl. Mix in shallot, parsley, chives, pickle, lemon juice, sea salt, and pepper. Let marinate for 5 minutes before serving.

NUTRITION FACTS:

133 calories; protein 14.3g; carbohydrates 0.6g; fat 7.7g;

TUNA TARTARE

Prep:
10 mins
Total:
10 mins
Servings:
6
Yield:
6 servings

INGREDIENTS:

1 pound sushi grade tuna, finely diced
3 tablespoons olive oil
¼ teaspoon wasabi powder
1 tablespoon sesame seeds
⅛ teaspoon cracked black pepper
sliced French bread

DIRECTIONS:

1
In a bowl, stir together olive oil, wasabi powder, sesame seeds, and cracked black pepper. Toss tuna into mixture until evenly coated. Adjust seasoning as desired with additional wasabi powder or black pepper. Serve on sliced French bread.

NUTRITION FACTS:
366 calories; protein 26.7g; carbohydrates 42.6g;

SUSHI RICE

Prep:
5 mins
Cook:
30 mins
Total:
35 mins
Servings:
3
Yield:
3 cups

INGREDIENTS:

2 cups water
1 teaspoon salt
1 teaspoon sugar
½ sheet nori (dry seaweed)
1 cup uncooked glutinous white rice (sushi rice)

DIRECTIONS:

1

In a saucepan, combine the water, salt, sugar and nori. Bring to a boil and add the rice. Cover, set heat to low and simmer for 20 minutes.

NUTRITION FACTS:

234 calories; protein 4.2g; carbohydrates 51.8g; fat 0.3g;

CHICKEN KATSU

Prep:
10 mins
Cook:
10 mins
Total:
20 mins
Servings:
4
Yield:
4 servings

INGREDIENTS:

4 skinless, boneless chicken breast halves - pounded to 1/2 inch thickness
salt and pepper to taste
2 tablespoons all-purpose flour
1 egg, beaten
1 cup panko bread crumbs
1 cup oil for frying, or as needed

DIRECTIONS:

1
Season the chicken breasts on both sides with salt and pepper. Place the flour, egg and panko crumbs into separate shallow dishes. Coat the chicken breasts in flour, shaking off any excess. Dip them into the egg, and then press into the panko crumbs until well coated on both sides.

2
Heat 1/4 inch of oil in a large skillet over medium-high heat. Place chicken in the hot oil, and cook 3 or 4 minutes per side, or until golden brown.

NUTRITION FACTS:

297 calories; protein 31.2g; carbohydrates 22.2g; fat 11.4g;

NORI SOUP

Prep:
15 mins
Cook:
18 mins
Total:
33 mins
Servings:
6
Yield:
6 servings

INGREDIENTS:

1 pound ground pork
2 quarts water
1 cube chicken bouillon
1 (8 ounce) can sliced water chestnuts
3 sheets nori (dry seaweed), broken into pieces.
1 egg, beaten
½ teaspoon salt
4 green onions, chopped
¾ teaspoon sesame oil

DIRECTIONS:

1

In a large saucepan over medium-high heat, cook the ground pork until browned. Drain off excess fat, and add water. Bring to a boil, then reduce heat to medium, and simmer uncovered for 15 minutes.

2

Stir in the bouillon cube to dissolve, and add water chestnuts and nori. Stir in the egg, and season with salt. Remove from heat, and mix in the green onions and sesame oil. Serve immediately

NUTRITION FACTS:

196 calories; protein 15.2g; carbohydrates 5.6g; fat 12.4g;

Nigiri academy

CHAPTER 3: STAPLES AND SAUCE

EEL SAUCE

Prep:
5 mins
Cook:
10 mins
Total:
15 mins
Servings:
6
Yield:
3/4 cup

INGREDIENTS:

½ cup soy sauce
½ cup white sugar
½ cup mirin (Japanese sweet wine)

DIRECTIONS:

1

Heat soy sauce, sugar, and mirin into a small saucepan over medium heat. Cook and stir until liquid is reduced to about 3/4 cup.

NUTRITION FACTS:

121 calories; protein 1.4g; carbohydrates 24.5g;

TEMPURA DIPPING SAUCE

Cook:
5 mins
Total:
5 mins
Servings:
4
Yield:
4 servings

INGREDIENTS:

1 cup water
1 tablespoon dashi granules
¼ cup mirin (Japanese sweet wine)
2 tablespoons soy sauce

DIRECTIONS:

1
In a small saucepan, bring water to a boil. Stir in dashi, and cook for 2 minutes. Remove from heat, and stir in mirin and soy sauce.

NUTRITION FACTS:

38 calories; protein 0.6g; carbohydrates 5.3g; sodium 452.8mg.

SWEET AND SOUR SAUCE

Prep:
2 mins
Cook:
10 mins
Total:
12 mins
Servings:
16
Yield:
2 cups

INGREDIENTS:

¾ cup white sugar
⅓ cup white vinegar
⅔ cup water
¼ cup soy sauce
1 tablespoon ketchup
2 tablespoons cornstarch

DIRECTIONS:

1
Place the sugar, vinegar, water, soy sauce, ketchup and cornstarch in a medium saucepan, and bring to a boil. Stir continuously until the mixture has thickened.

NUTRITION FACTS:
43 calories; protein 0.3g; carbohydrates 10.8g;

PEANUT SAUCE

Prep:
10 mins
Total:
10 mins
Servings:
5
Yield:
4 to 6 servings

INGREDIENTS:

1 cup natural peanut butter
1 cup hot water
½ cup distilled white vinegar
¼ cup tamari
¼ cup molasses
1 teaspoon ground cayenne pepper

DIRECTIONS:

1
In a small saucepan, whisk together peanut butter and water over low heat. Stir in vinegar, tamari, molasses, and cayenne pepper. Heat through, but do not simmer or boil; cooking can cause the sauce to curdle.

NUTRITION FACTS:

375 calories; protein 14.6g; carbohydrates 25g; fat 27.1g

HOMEMADE PICKLED GINGER

Prep:
40 mins
Cook:
5 mins
Total:
45 mins
Servings:
32
Yield:
1 1/2 cups

INGREDIENTS:

8 ounces fresh young ginger root, peeled
1 ½ teaspoons sea salt
1 cup rice vinegar
⅓ cup white sugar

DIRECTIONS:

1

Cut the ginger into chunks and place them into a bowl. Sprinkle with sea salt, stir to coat and let stand for about 30 minutes. Transfer the ginger to a clean jar.

2

In a saucepan, stir together the rice vinegar and sugar until sugar has dissolved. Bring to a boil, then pour the boiling liquid over the ginger root pieces in the jar.

3

Allow the mixture to cool, then put the lid on the jar and store in the refrigerator for at least one week. You will see that the liquid will change to slightly pinkish in few minutes. Don't be alarmed because it's the reaction of rice vinegar that causes the change. Only quality rice vinegar can do that! Some commercial pickled ginger has red coloring added. Cut pieces of ginger into paper thin slices for serving.

NUTRITION FACTS:

14 calories; protein 0.1g; carbohydrates 3.3g; fat 0.1g; sodium 83.4mg

Japanese Yellow Sauce

Prep:
10 mins
Additional:
30 mins
Total:
40 mins
Servings:
16
Yield:
16 servings

INGREDIENTS:

1 cup mayonnaise
3 tablespoons white sugar
3 tablespoons vinegar
2 tablespoons melted butter
1 teaspoon tomato paste
¾ teaspoon paprika
¼ teaspoon cayenne pepper, or to taste
¼ teaspoon garlic powder, or to taste

DIRECTIONS:

1
Mix mayonnaise, sugar, vinegar, butter, tomato paste, paprika, cayenne pepper, and garlic powder together in a bowl until smooth; refrigerate until chilled, at least 30 minutes.

NUTRITION FACTS:

121 calories; protein 0.2g; carbohydrates 3g; fat 12.4g; cholesterol 9mg;

www.ingramcontent.com/pod-product-compliance
Lightning Source LLC
Chambersburg PA
CBHW081417080526
44589CB00016B/2575